JAN CARLIE

INSTAGRAM STORIES

**The Ultimate Guide on Instagram Stories, Learn How
It Works Plus Tips and Tricks on What Content to Posts
and How You Can Monetize Your Instagram Account**

Descrierea CIP a Bibliotecii Naţionale a României
JAN CARLIE
   INSTAGRAM STORIES. The Ultimate Guide on Instagram Stories, Learn How It Works Plus Tips and Tricks on What Content to Posts and How You Can Monetize Your Instagram Account / Jan Carlie – Bucharest: Editura My Ebook, 2021
   ISBN

JAN CARLIE

INSTAGRAM STORIES

The Ultimate Guide on Instagram Stories, Learn How It Works Plus Tips and Tricks on What Content to Posts and How You Can Monetize Your Instagram Account

My Ebook Publishing House
Bucharest, 2021

CONTENTS

Chapter 1

Introducing Instagram

Instagram is often described as being 'Twitter' with images and this is largely a fair description of what the social media platform does and how it works. But to say that that is *all* Instagram is would be a big disservice. Instagram is actually an incredibly powerful tool, a highly nuanced platform and something that deserves a big place in every single internet marketing campaign.

And now, Instagram has added to its roster of capabilities even further with its awesome 'stories' function. Instagram has gone from being an indispensable and highly underused tool for engaging with an audience and establishing authority, to being something even *more* powerful – an opportunity to bring your fans along with you and to let them feel like they're really a part of your brand.

In this book, we'll be taking an in-depth look at Instagram and at how you can use it, along with all of its most modern features, in order to build massive trust and influence and have a huge impact on your audience. At the same time, we'll be taking a more in-depth look specifically at Instagram stories. You'll see why this is an *incredibly* important addition from a marketing perspective and how you can start using it right away to make the biggest impact possible.

Why Instagram Matters

Instagram will often be relegated to 'afterthought' in a number of internet marketing campaigns. If you have an ebook or a blog to promote, then there's a good chance that you will have thought long and hard about how you're going to handle your SEO and how you're going to dominate Facebook; but won't have given much consideration at all to how you're going to kill it on Instagram.

This of course is a big mistake, as you will learn in this chapter.

In fact, you only need to take a look at how *other* brands are treating Instagram in order to see why it's such a big deal...

And what you will find when you do look into this, is that an *awful* lot of money is spent on Instagram. There are countless brands that are spending large amounts of cash investing in influencers, or becoming influencers themselves. Many particularly savvy individuals have even managed to make a full-time living on Instagram by getting high paying sponsors to support their channel.

Brands are willing to support channels in this way because they know what a massive impact Instagram can have on an audience. Instagram is not only impressive in terms of the numbers but also the engagement and the way it is able to 'sell a dream'. Like they say: a picture tells a thousand words. Add some impressive filters and your word count goes up big time!

Instagram in Numbers

Instagram in Numbers

And while you might not think of Instagram right away as one of the 'main' social media channels... well, you should really think again! Instagram actually has an incredible 500 million users, which is 1 million more than last year! That makes it the *second* largest social media platform just behind Facebook – it is actually *bigger* than Twitter!

What's more, is that Instagram is growing faster than the majority of other platforms. It does appear to be *somewhat* slowing down in the growth department but it is still a juggernaut with incredible momentum when compared with other platforms.

Instagram also has more monthly advertisers than Twitter and engagement is also particularly high. Instagram has over 500 million active monthly users and those users have shared over 40 billion photos in total. That's 95 million photos and videos each day!

Instagram also has some other very appealing statistics behind it. For instance, it is one of the very best platforms for reaching women. In fact, 31% of *all* American women use Instagram (compared with 24% of all American men). This is a great opportunity for brands that are marketing their goods to women then and it also has a particularly international audience – with 80% of users being outside the US.

A survey conducted by Iconosquare in 2015 revealed that 70% of users have at some point sought out a brand to follow on Instagram. 62% have followed brands they love and 41% are open to marketing messages and discounts. 65% of users also reported that they found it flattering when a brand liked their post.

All this engagement sounds great on paper but it's even better when you compare it with other platforms. Instagram – according to research firm L2 – actually has 18 times more engagement than Facebook or Twitter.

From your standpoint as an advertiser, Instagram also has a lot of advantages: one being the fact that it is so quick and convenient to use. The great thing about Instagram is that all you have to do is point a camera phone and shoot – there's no need to come up with a witty comment or a good idea! Posting to Instagram is fast then but it can have *massive* impact – this translates to incredible ROI.

What You Will Learn

What You Will Learn

In this book, we'll be taking a deep dive into Instagram and particularly into the latest feature: Instagram Stories. You'll learn how Instagram works, how to make the very most of its different features and how to leverage these – as well as Instagram Stories – to make a MASSIVE impact on a huge audience.

Instagram really does have the power to transform your brand and to drive massive sales, you just need to know how to make the very most of it. Read this book and you'll learn just that.

A small selection of the things we'll cover includes…

- A rundown of Instagram's features and history
- How to create stunning images and photos that really grab attention

- How to build and grow your audience to incredible heights
- How to ensure maximum engagement
- How to drive sales and downloads from your account
- How to use live video and Instagram Stories in order to create an even more powerful relationship with your viewers
- How to monetize your Instagram account
- How to integrate Instagram with your other social media activities and internet marketing strategies
- How to attract and acquire sponsors to earn a living *solely* from Instagram
- And much more!

Chapter 2

Instagram's History and Features

Instagram was created by Kevin Systrom and Mike Krieger and first went live in October 2010 as a mobile app. The basic premise is very simple. Instagram allows you to upload a photo to your own profile and to view photos that others have uploaded on a feed. The objective here is different from Facebook however. Rather than keeping an archive of all your photos in order to tell your own story; the objective with Instagram is rather to be more selective. You will generally upload a single photo at a time and spend a little time cropping it, adding filters and generally making it look as artistic as possible.

Instagram has since been described by many as an opportunity to find art in everyday moments. You'll see pictures of empty gyms, of wine glasses with lipstick stains, of sunsets, of running shoes covered in mud – all with different filters applied and a story to tell. Those who understand the platform well manage to create some very artistic images using only very limited tools.

Those tools are 'filters'. These are simple effects that can be applied to Instagram images, in order to give them a retro look, different colour temperatures, faded effects and much more.

It took no time at all for the service to grow to 100 million users by April 2012 and 300 million by December 2014. This is unheard of growth in the industry and as such, it was only a matter of time before Facebook would come knocking and make an acquisition. Facebook demonstrated tremendous faith in the platform when, in April 2012, it purchased Instagram for a whopping US $1 million (cash and stock). This would prove to be a smart move – while Instagram grew by 23% over the following year, Facebook would only grow by 3% during the same timeframe.

Facebook made a promise to Instagram users at the time not to ruin the platform with new features or to be too intrusive. For the most part, the company has been true to its word and it would certainly be fair to say that Instagram has maintained its integrity and core purpose over the years. Instagram has been somewhat integrated into Facebook but not to a huge degree; if you did not know that the two were owned by the same company, then you could very realistically not realise it on looks alone.

That said, there have still been a large number of different changes and updates to Instagram over the years and these have largely improved the platform. For instance, Instagram would originally only support a square image format in order to mimic old Polaroid photos. Later, it would introduce the ability to upload photos in a range of aspect ratios, creating many more possibilities over time.

Another perhaps overdue feature that was added in 2013 was video sharing. Users could record and share videos up to 15 seconds and with resolutions of 640x640. This was seen by some as an attempt to compete with other platforms that revolved around video sharing – such as vine. However, it was arguably a logical addition to the platform's roster of features.

Then came more precise editing controls. Rather than just being able to add different filters, users could now alter different settings manually – controlling things like the brightness, the contrast, the saturation etc.

Instagram Direct was also added in 2013 and was another important upgrade. This allowed users to send images directly to other users. In 2015, new features were added to this mode, allowing for basic instant messaging and the ability to share multiple photos at once. The main function for this however is of course to share pictures that you think a friend or a contact will particularly enjoy.

And then came Instagram stories…

Instagram Stories

Instagram Stories was added on August 2nd 2016 and at the time of writing, it is the newest *big* addition to Instagram's functionality. It's also one of the biggest game-changers for the platform and very much a product of its time.

Essentially, Instagram Stories allows users to add images and videos for their followers to see and that will disappear after 24 hours. These images don't appear on the user's profile grid on the feed and also allow for the inclusion of Live Video –

which are Live Streamed videos that can last for up to one hour. Live video uses the same interface as the stories option but will self destruct instantly once they're over.

Instagram Stories has a lot of potential for marketers and has many unique benefits outside of the main features of Instagram. The first reason for this, is that Instagram Stories appear in a different place to the other content on Instagram. These appear in small circles along the top of a feed, thereby drawing a lot more attention to themselves and at the same time increasing engagement.

The other reason that Instagram Stories are so successful and one of the reasons they are so much a product of their time, is that they can be likened to various forms of live content.

Right now, live content is all the rage. This was a big deal in 2015 and 2016 with the likes of Periscope and Meerkat. These were two massive 'live streaming' apps that enabled users to broadcast videos live to a global audience. These videos could be recorded and would then remain on the channel for a while for those who missed them. But the most exciting part of these platforms is being able to look at the world map (in Periscope at least) and tune in to all the people broadcasting live from anywhere in the world. You can see behind-the-scenes from live News broadcasts, you can see people vlogging from their kitchens over their morning cup of coffee and you can see people working out live.

Live video has a much more intimate and immediate effect and it allows creators to interact directly with their audience. Most live video solutions allow for some form of commenting and this means that the broadcaster can then respond live to the audience.

Imagine the benefit as a product manufacturer of being able to demo your product live on air and then answer questions about it in real time.

Imagine the power of being able to chat with your fans live and let them feel like they're coming with you as you carry out your daily chores! Imagine how much more engaged they would be and how this could help to turn them into *even bigger* fans!

Snapchat has a similar appeal. Snapchat is not 'live' for the most part but it nevertheless allows you to share photos directly with an audience from anywhere that are very 'in the moment' in nature (Snapchat images self-destruct). This has proven highly popular and has seen Snapchat continue to grow and exceed expectations despite everything.

People *love* feeling as though they have intimate, privileged access to their very favourite creators.

So it was only a matter of time before other platforms began to follow suit. First we saw Facebook join in the party with Facebook Live. Now Instagram is doing the very same thing.

Instagram Stories is essentially 'Snapchat on Instagram'.

And the live video function marries this perfectly with Periscope and Facebook Live-type functionality.

Take the already huge potential of Instagram and introduce these two very exciting and very current features and you have a recipe for something truly huge.

And THIS is exactly why Instagram Stories is such big news for marketers…

Chapter 3

Getting Started With Instagram –
Choosing a Niche and Setting Up

Before you can start to make a massive splash on Instagram Stories though, you first need to get started with regular old Instagram.

And now it's time to reveal the power of Instagram and how you can tap into it. It's time to learn what it is about Instagram that makes massive stars and just why brands are willing to invest so much of their money into it…

Selling the Dream

In business, there is a very useful term that it pays to understand. That term is 'Value Proposition'.

The value proposition is the way in which you are claiming to offer value to your users. This means that you're asking what it is about your products, your services or your content that makes people interested. How do their lives stand to improve through their interaction with you?

This is all about understanding that the total should always be more than the sum of its parts.

In other words, you are not selling the brick and mortar – the physical materials that go into the creation of your product.

If you are selling a book on getting fit, then you are not really selling a book on fitness.

Rather, you are selling fitness itself. You are selling the feeling of having amazing abs. Of knowing that you look great when you take your top off. Of knowing that you are desirable.

You are selling the feeling of waking up first thing in the morning full of energy and ready to go.

You are selling the feeling of looking *great* in your clothes. Of taking up physical space thanks to your muscle. Of walking into a room and making an impression and turning heads.

Those are all amazing things to be able to sell someone and your audience will be willing to pay a *big* price for that.

The same goes for business consultancy. You aren't just selling information: you're selling the dream of running a highly successful business: of wearing slick suits, of having employees and of knowing that what you're doing is important.

Your value proposition is your 'dream'. It's the dream that people are willing to pay money for and it's the dream that will set your business apart from the competition. The dream is what will turn followers into true fans and what will get you likes and shares and follows.

And Instagram is *all about* selling dreams.

Remember what we said earlier: Instagram is about finding art in everyday activities. It's about taking something that is relatively dull and making it seem incredibly exciting.

People will often follow others on Instagram because they want to live vicariously and to be inspired.

Examples of Highly Effective Insta-gram Accounts

Examples of Highly Effective Instagram Accounts

Take a look at some of the most popular fitness brands and how they operate. These channels work by posting images of a perfect fitness lifestyle. You'll see silhouettes of people running against a sunset along a beach. You'll see pictures of incredibly ripped guys standing over weights with chalk in their hands.

You'll see pictures of incredibly fit women with perfectly formed rears in the squatting rack.

All of these things paint a picture that is highly desirable for anyone who wishes they were a bit fitter. They love looking at these images – especially if they aren't that happy with their own fitness - because they find them inspiring and because they like to imagine that one day their lives will be like that.

That's also why fashion is so popular on Instagram. There are countless female Instagram stars who post pictures of themselves in highly form-fitting outfits, looking absolutely stunning and thereby making other women highly jealous (of course they also tend to have a few male followers as well!).

And can you imagine what kind of position that puts these women in when it comes to promoting products? With all those followers who wish their lives were just like those women's, their ability to promote a product is of course almost unparalleled!

Another very popular type of account is the 'Battlestation' channel. Battlestations are essentially set- ups for gaming PCs or productivity stations. These are super powerful desktop PCs with advanced lighting set-ups, multi-monitor arrays, keyboards with insane lighting and awesome pop-culture décor. Again, people like to follow these channels as fans of tech because they can use them for ideas, inspiration and a little bit of lust.

What about food porn? These accounts literally just take photos of beautiful looking meals and combine this with recipe advice, or reviews of places to eat. Again though, this appeals to the kind of person who loves cooking and loves eating and who gets a real kick out of making something delicious or finding those hidden indie places to eat.

Travel is another area that lends itself very naturally to these kinds of channels and it's not uncommon to see people posting pictures of themselves in front of lots of exotic locations.

While they come in many different forms, the best Instagram accounts are all about promoting a way of life, a movement or a dream – and that is where the incredible engagement comes from.

An Extreme Example

If you want an example of how Instagram can work in the extreme, then consider 'stunting'. Stunting is the somewhat strange practice of essentially pretending that you have more money than you do, or that you live an incredibly rich lifestyle.

A typical example might be to take a photo of your own hand on a car steering wheel. That car is of course a Lamborghini and just to complete the image, you are also wearing a Rolex. Other people will withdraw lots of their own cash, so they can lie in bed along with lots of piles of it, or they will take photos of themselves on first class flights (when actually they were just passing through to go to the toilet).

People who wish they were better off and who dream of this kind of lifestyle will then often follow those accounts, just so that they can live vicariously and imagine that it is them with all that money. Sometimes, they will even *know* that the 'stunter' is faking it and won't even care because they are just happy to see those images and to pretend along with the creator.

It's a strange practice but it just shows the magic of Instagram and what a powerful impact that can have...

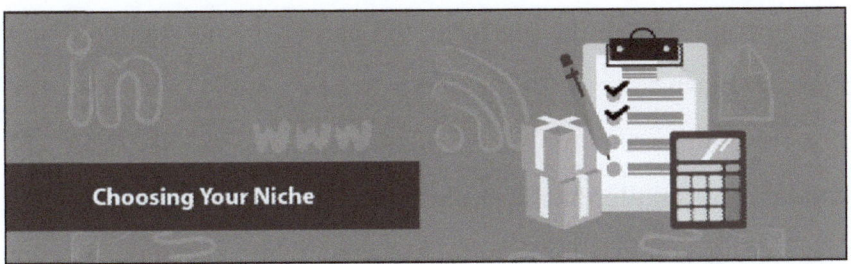

Choosing Your Niche

To get started then and to start doing the same, you're going to first have to choose the niche you want to focus on. A niche of course is a subject matter and it can also mean your industry. A niche means more than that though because it also defines who your audience is, what the value proposition is and more.

As you can imagine, certain niches will lend themselves a little better to Instagram than others. We've seen just how effective fitness can be as a niche and how other things like fashion, food and more all work well too.

Of course though, it can pay to try and avoid competing directly within a massive niche. While it is still outlandishly high, engagement has been going *down* somewhat on Instagram as numbers have risen and the obvious reason for that, is that the more people are on the platform, the harder it is to stand out and make a splash.

If you want to sidestep direct competition, then try choosing a smaller niche within the broader category. So for instance, if you are going to tackle fitness, then you can always try going with something slightly different or more specific – like fitness for the elderly, outdoor fitness, weight lifting, calisthenics etc.

Likewise, if you are going to choose 'fashion', then maybe you could focus more on plus side fashion, on retro fashion, on 'fashion on a budget' etc. By giving your brand something more distinct to help it stand out, you will find that more people want to follow you and that you make a bigger impact as a result.

For Existing Brands

Of course, there's a good chance that you already *have* your brand and that you're just looking for a way to promote that brand *through* Instagram. In this case, you want to consider how you can take whatever your industry or niche is and then make it into something a little more visual and inspiring.

For example, if you happen to be in Life Insurance, then you might be wondering just how you can make that as inspiring and visual as something like fitness. The good news is that there *is* a way – you just need to choose a theme that is highly related, that will appeal to the precise same audience, but that isn't necessarily directly the same as your product.

Ask yourself: what is the value proposition of your business and how can you portray that in a visual way?

There are essentially two value propositions when it comes to life insurance. Those are:

- Looking after your family
- Improving your finances

You can focus on either of these for your Instagram account. Either you could post lots of pictures of happy families in nice houses doing things together, or you could post lots of pictures related to money saving and living a cost-effective lifestyle.

Either of these accounts would give people a good reason to follow and would potentially be inspiring but neither is *directly* on the nose.

Another option is to choose a 'personal brand'. A personal brand is essentially where you take your own persona and make that into an indistinguishable part of your company. You become the public face and you bond with your audience by allowing them to feel as though they are getting to know you.

In many ways, Richard Branson is a personal brand. Likewise, you can also think of a lot of top bloggers and vloggers (think PewDiePie or Tim Ferriss) as being personal brands.

The great thing about a personal brand is that people become fans of *you* and not just the product or service that you're promoting. From there, it is then your job to demonstrate that you 'live what you preach'. Your personal brand and your lifestyle match what your product is about.

So if you have a blog about fitness and you have a personal brand, then your posts can be of you working out, of you eating healthy meals, of you going on healthy walks... etc.

But the difference here is that you're also going to occasionally include photos that are more related to your personal life: maybe photos of you out and about with your friends, or photos of your other hobbies or your dog. If you get this right and if you've built enough of a relationship with your followers, then they will like getting these insights into your life and they will all become part of your image.

Note that a personal brand works very well for Instagram Stories which have that very personal and intimate feel. If you don't currently have a personal brand, then you might want to consider exposing yourself a little more to your audience for the purposes of this new tool.

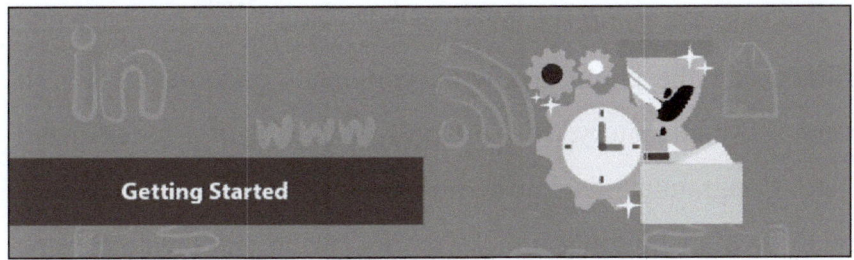

Getting Started

Once you've chosen how you're going to approach Instagram, all that is left to do is to get started with an account.

For all of the recent additions and innovations to Instagram, one thing is missing: and that is the inclusion of any kind of website. While there is a website to be found (www.instagram.com), it is very limited in scope. You can scroll through your homefeed on here and you can like photos and videos. What you can't do though, is to upload photos.

For that, you're going to need the phone app for iOS, Android or Windows Phone. Using this, you'll be able to sign up and create an account (or use your existing Facebook account) and from there, posting photos is a simple matter of hitting the 'Plus' icon in the middle down the bottom and then choosing a photo from your gallery or taking a new one with the camera. There's also the option to record a new video here.

Once the photo is taken or uploaded, you can then add filters, edit the photo and write comments underneath. It's all very self-explanatory, so we won't go into it in a lot of detail here. Congratulations, you're now on Instagram and you're now ready to start building a massive following and creating some real trust and influence!

Chapter 4

How to Grow Your Account

If you have followed the advice in the last chapter, then you should have a great value proposition and really be promoting an idealized lifestyle that you hope to offer people through your services or products. This alone should be enough to give your account some real momentum. Also important is to make sure that your photos and videos are of a high standard. This is something that we'll look at in a lot more detail in a subsequent chapter but for now, suffice to say that people won't follow a channel if it is low quality!

But that's not *all* you need to do. You can have the best account in the world but if you don't know how to promote it, then people aren't going to see your pictures *or* your Instagram Stories. In this chapter then, we'll be looking at what you can do to solve that problem and to make sure that people discover your channel and sign up in their droves!

Growing an Instagram Account, the Basics

Growing an Instagram Account, the Basics

The first thing you need to do to ensure that your Instagram account will grow quickly, is to post content consistently. That means you need to be consistent in terms of the frequency of your posting *and* in terms of the nature of the posting. People need to learn what they can expect from your account, so that they can make the decision whether or not to follow you.

If you created the personal brand as mentioned in the last chapter, then it's okay to be a little bit looser in terms of what you post. But if you have a fitness brand and all you ever post are pictures of your dogs, then you're going to lose your followers. Likewise, if you have a productivity brand and you fill it with images of yourself travelling, you will lose fans.

So be consistent and make sure that you are posting relevant content at least daily – ideally a lot more than that.

You also need to do whatever else you can do to help people know what your brand is all about. One of your most powerful tools in this respect will be your logo and your brand name. If you have an account all about fitness, then you need a logo and a name that will communicate this as soon as people see it. You want your first-time viewers to instantly know what you're all about so that they can decide then and there that they want to follow you and that your content is for them.

How to Gain Followers

But how do you get people to see your content in the first place at all? There are a few different methods you can use:

Interact With Others: Remember that Instagram is a social media platform. And what is social media? It's a communication tool! So if you aren't using Instagram for communication, then you aren't using it the way it is designed and you aren't making the most of it!

One very easy to help more people find your content, is to look for the content that others are sharing and then to comment on it or like it. We've already seen that people find this flattering and if you think about your own reaction to that, chances are that you would want to check out just who it was who liked you.

So search for different tags and see what other people are contributing. If you post about fitness a lot, then how about searching for the tag 'fitness', seeing what other people have contributed and then leaving some comments on those posts. They'll check you out to see what you're all about and if they find a ton of amazing photos that appeal to them, chances are that they'll follow you!

Likewise, spend some time liking other photos and just generally *using* the platform.

The thing you *mustn't* do? Post on someone else's image and say 'Please check out my profile!'. All this does is make you look desperate and amateurish – and it is invasive because you are taking someone's photo and just using it as an excuse to promote your own nonsense.

Always comment on the content of the picture and leave relevant feedback so that it's clear you're actually engaging and not just a bot posting random compliments.

Another thing *not* to do is to tag people in your photos who aren't really in them. This is immensely frustrating and once again just *cheap* – it will undermine the quality of your brand.

Integration: Another way to bring more new people to your Instagram account is to integrate it with your other channels and accounts. One of the most effective ways to do this is through your own website or blog and if you have a WordPress site, then you can use a variety of powerful tools to integrate your Instagram into it.

One thing I have done for instance, is to add a feed from my Instagram into the right hand column of my website. That way, someone who lands on my website will be able to see the kind of thing I post on Instagram and then decide to follow me then and there. It also has the added advantage of keeping my website up-to-date with a constant stream of new content. Even when I haven't been on my website for a while, it will look alive with content and new updates and it makes my visitors feel like they know me that bit better, thereby establishing trust.

I also have buttons on my homepage that show people where they can follow me on Instagram and my other social media. Again, that means that if they enjoy the content on my site, they know how to follow me on Instagram.

What's more though, is that I regularly just *ask* my fans to follow me. At the ends of posts and at the end of YouTube videos, I'll say 'check out my Instagram account for more fitness inspiration' etc. This is a great way to draw attention to it and to make sure that it doesn't get overlooked.

Another useful strategy is to use IFTTT and the sharing buttons within Instagram to post your content to your other social media accounts. For example, you can set it up so that any new picture added to Instagram will automatically be posted to your Twitter account as well as your Facebook page. That way, people who aren't following you on Instagram will still be impressed by your content and they'll get taken to your Instagram account if they click to enlarge the image.

Tags: Another very powerful tool for growing your following on Instagram is to use tags correctly. Tags work just the same as they do in Twitter, you add them in your comments section beneath any new picture and other users will then be able to search for them in order to see what new content has been posted on that subject.

So if you were to use Instagram's search function right now and to look for 'Makeup', then you would find countless recent pictures uploaded by women showing off their makeup. Many of these would link you to YouTube accounts and websites filled with makeup tutorials and if you were into that sort of thing, then you might follow them. The same goes for 'fitness' and 'productivity'.

Except it is a mistake to use those tags. Why? Because there are *so* many people who will search for these tags and who will take new photos. If you tag an image with 'Fitness', it will instantly be drowned by hundreds of thousands of new photos and no one will see it.

On the other hand though, if you tag something with 'morningrun', then it might get a few more searches and get seen a few more times before it gets completely buried.

Your aim in general then, is to use tags that are popular but not so popular as to make it impossible to stand out. And of course, the way you make a tag is simply to add a '#' symbol in front of something before you post it.

Influencer Marketing: One of THE most powerful ways to massively explode your channel on Instagram is to use influencer marketing. This essentially means that you're going to contact someone who is *already* highly popular on Instagram and then you're going to try and convince them to promote you in some way. You might find a prominent fitness model then and ask them if they would consider sharing one of your images and linking to your account in the comments. That way, you gain instant access to a huge proportion of the people that they have access to.

Don't go straight for the biggest creators on Instagram with a million followers or they likely won't answer you (they get a *lot* of messages in all likelihood!). Instead, look for someone who is just that little bit bigger than you – someone that you can stand to gain from but that is still small enough that they might be flattered that you contacted them.

You can also aim for big brands that are running competitions and other promotions themselves. For instance, many big channels will repost photos taken by their favourite Instagram contributors and this is a way that they encourage people to use their tags. You can do the same and if your photo gets selected, then that will give you access to a big audience once again.

One thing to *never* do though is to buy followers. Not only will the quality of the followers you buy be very low (meaning that they won't be engaged with your brand, if they look at your posts at all!) but it will also be likely to backfire as this is against Instagram's policies and you could find your account being suspended…

Chapter 5

How to Use Instagram Stories

Now you are up to speed with how to create a successful Instagram account that will have real clout and that will really grow your audience, it's time to think about how you're going to integrate Instagram's latest and most exciting new features.

So how exactly do you use Instagram Stories?

Instagram Stories: The Basics

Instagram Stories: The Basics

Instagram is quite a simple tool, which is actually one of its strongest selling points. However, by adding Instagram stories, it has added a lot more functionality and the UI doesn't quite lend itself to this yet. Suffice to say that it is a little less intuitive than a lot of the other functionality, which may even have contributed to the slight slowing of new user adoption – is it less easy to pick up and play now?

Whatever the case, this chapter will walk you through it, so you'll be good to go! To get started...

1. First, right click on the plus icon that is found at the top left of the home screen. This will be next to the other stories and it will say 'My Story' next to it with your profile images.You can also click on the Instagram icon above and to the left, depending on your version and your region. You can also launch this by just swiping left from the main feed, or by swiping right from the homescreen (like I said, not entirely intuitive...).

2. Now tap the circle bottom that is found at the bottom of the screen in order to take a photo. Or you can tap and hold if you want to record a video.

3. From there, you can then edit the photos or videos as you normally would in Instagram, or you can draw or write on the screen just like you would if you were using Snapchat (there are a LOT of similarities here in fact...). To add filters,

you simply swipe across it and there will be seven to pick from (less than usual, though we suspect more are on the way).

4. Badges again work like Snapchat and allow for a little more editing in your images. A cool trick that some Instagram creators are using is to use the polka dot image in order to create thought bubble effects.

5. You can also tag people in your stories using the @symbol as you normally would. They will be alerted in Instagram direct and can then check out the story.

Tap 'Done' to save your story and then tap the check-mark button the share it.

Note that your stories will work a little differently to your regularly pictures. Remember, these will only last for 24 hours, so if your followers miss them, they will disappear. That does also mean that they aren't added to your grid on your profile and this is one of the advantages – it's easier to post something a little more 'off message' here: perhaps something that is a bit of fun.

Each time you add a new photo, it will be added to your story and your fans will be able to watch those images and videos in a slideshow.

Remember: your stories will appear at the top of the homefeed and will be indicated by a red ring circling your profile picture. Users who want to view your stories can then click on that image and will be able to sit back and watch the slide show, or swipe through images in order to speed it along.

Going Live

If you want to go live, then this will work just a little bit differently. All you need to do is open up the stories camera by swiping or clicking the plus button and then select the 'Live' option. This is found along the bottom next to the 'Normal' and 'Boomerang' options. A live tag will now appear on your Instagram Stories bubble, so that followers will know that they can tap it in order to see what you're doing live. Your video will then disappear though, so make sure that you are careful to choose whether you would rather make a live video, a contribution to your story or a regular video upload!

Something else neat about going live is that your followers will be notified even when they're not on Instagram (unless they have actively turned this off). This increases engagement and it's a great way to get people to join in with whatever you're doing and to increase engagement and trust that way.

At any time you can click to rotate the camera and if you select the 'Hands Free' option, then you'll be able to record without holding down the button. This is useful for recording workouts or other things where you want to be in the shot and not talking to the selfie camera.

During Your Live Videos

During your live videos, you will notice comments appearing down the bottom if you are getting good engagement. These are the people who are watching your video right now and you'll also be able to reply to the comments.

But why reply to the comments by typing when you have the option to reply to the comments by voice? If someone asks a question, then just answer that question in person and while chatting.

You'll also be able to see people appearing and disappearing in the live video and this is a good way to get more engagement – when you see someone join your chat, then why not welcome them and ask them how they are? The first time you start watching a live video and this happens it feels very weird and it really shows the power of being live in a big way!

Making Boomerangs

You may notice that next to the Live option is another option called 'Boomerangs'. This is another new feature which is quite interesting and is essentially a very short, looping video. It works a lot like a GIF or perhaps the Live Photos from the iPhone 6S.

Once in the Stories camera, simply click on the capture button and a burst of 10 photos will be taken automatically and stitched together into a 1 second video. This can then be played normally or in reverse. You can share these on Instagram, in your stories or even on Facebook and elsewhere. They look pretty cool and are certainly a good way to demonstrate tech savvy on your account.

Tips, Tricks and Hidden Settings

There are a few more tips, tricks and hidden settings that won't be immediately apparent when you first start using these new features.

For starters, it *is* possible to save your photos taken for the Instagram Stories. To do this, hit the settings button on the top left and then choose 'Save Shared Photos'. This will share your photos to your device, which is handy because you can then make use of them elsewhere, or just keep them for your own amusement.

It's also possible to do the reverse and to share your Snapchat photos in your Instagram Stories, thereby getting more use out of them. Reusing content is just *smart* if you are an internet marketing or social media marketer! To download Snapchat photos, all you need to do is click the 'Download Button'.

Note that you *cannot* however download any videos that are made live.

Security

Security and privacy is always important, even when you are a marketer and your aim is to reach as many people as possible.

For instance, you might not want your Mum to see your modelling shoot on Instagram and you may want to remove haters from your live video. Instagram has thought of both these things.

To prevent comments on live video for instance, you can simply turn the comments *off* from the settings menu.

Likewise, you can hide your stories from particular people through the settings menu. Go into the story settings again and then select 'Hide My Story From' and then choose who you want to exclude.

It is unfortunately impossible to comment on stories but what you can do is to message from them. Message a friend directly from their story by hitting 'Send Message' while viewing the story. You'll also be able to receive messages similarly when you broadcast your own. You'll need comments enabled to do this though.

Chapter 6

Making the Most of Instagram's Powerful New Features

Okay, so now you know just what Instagram's new features are all about and how to basically use them, it's time to start actually making the most of them! There's a big difference between using Instagram Stories and using them well...

Why We All Should be Excited by the Trend Toward Live

First though, we should look once again at just what makes Live and Stories so important...

If you are a cynical sort, then you might find yourself wondering just why live video has taken off in the way it has. What's all the fuss about? Is it just another trend that is likely to die of death in no time at all? Is it just marketing hype?

Actually, the reality of live video is quite a lot more impressive than even the hype would have you believe. Right now, different companies are clamouring to become the 'home' of live video streaming and there's a very good reason for that: it could very well change the world.

Imagine if live video caught on to such a degree that everyone started using it. Imagine if at any time, millions of people around the world were using their live video to share events. Imagine how this could change our understanding of the world.

Imagine if there was a natural disaster in a country where this had happened for instance. Forget news coverage: suddenly, the very best and most powerful way to learn about the disaster would be to tune in to all of the live footage being broadcast from friends, family, celebrities and strangers. It would be like virtual omnipresence – being able to see an event from countless different angles at once.

And once this happens, imagine how many *more* people will start using live video.

Live video essentially transports you to a place and time and it could change the way we consume news and media, the way we attend live events and more.

And when this integrates with other future technologies – such as virtual reality and 360 cameras – then we can really expect to start transport ourselves to wherever our friends are and to experience events as though we were there.

And from a marketing standpoint, being able to talk *directly* to your fans is unprecedented. Think of your favourite celebrity. Think about someone you really admire.

Now imagine if you knew they were going live and you could actually comment to them directly… they might even answer!

This is what you have the capability now to do – and your own fans will feel just as excited when *you* go live.

While Stories might not have the same potential, these too have the ability to potentially alter the way we interact with our fans – to let us bring them with us on our travels and to grow the trust in that relationship.

This is crucial when it comes to selling. Someone is going to be *much* more likely to want to buy from you once they feel as though they know you – when they've seen just how your ideas and services have helped you in your own life and once they've seen you playing with your dog or celebrating Christmas with your family.

How to Create Great Stories and Live Videos – Tips and Advice

The first challenge when it comes to creating great stories, is to know which of your videos and photos are going to lend themselves best to your stories versus your main Instagram.

Largely, the difference is whether you think of the photo as being quintessential to your brand and a great photo, or whether you think of it more as an aside – a little joke for the fans or a demonstration of something you've explained.

Likewise, more 'immediate' things work very well in your Stories, such as events.

Let's say you have a fitness channel for instance and you're at a Bodybuilding competition chatting with people on stalls and meeting fans. Photos of the actual show will look great on your channel, as these demonstrate what your brand is about and can be made to look dramatic and spectacular.

A photo of you with fans though, or of you getting a sausage roll from one of the stalls will work much better in your stories.

Meanwhile, video clips will work particularly well for the live video as they will give your audience a chance to attend along with you! Always be sure to check copyright though before you go ahead and stream or you can risk getting yourself into trouble.

If your brand does have a personal component, then as a rule, things that are your personal brand will work best for live or stories, whereas things that fit your corporate brand will work best on your grid as permanent additions.

Ask yourself: would you be happy for a photo to be a fan's first impression of your brand? If not, then it will work better as a story. The same goes for video, in which case you could share it live.

Content That is Great for Stories and Live

Content That is Great for Stories and Live

Certain content will of course lend itself particularly well to the Stories format or to being live. Here are some suggestions:

Stories

➢ As mentioned, photos with fans are great for stories

➢ Behind the scenes photos also work very well for stories and can be a great way to build anticipation for something. Got a new video in the works? Then why not post a photo of you filming or editing the video?

➢ Sequential photos – seeing as stories work like a slideshow, there are some fun effects you can pull off by uploading a few photos in a sequence. How about a few photos that show something you're cooking getting created?

➢ Photos that wouldn't be particularly attractive but that nevertheless fit your brand also work.

➢ You can also add photos that supplement the other photos you've taken. For instance, if you have taken 10 photos of the same activity, then you won't want to flood your account with them. Choose one or two for your grid and add the rest to your story.

➤ Stories are also a great place to shout out to another creator if you want to do a cross promotion!

➤ Jokes and funny asides also work great here!

Live Videos

➤ Travels – If you're travelling and you've come across something amazing, then why not let your followers come along with you for the ride?

➤ Events – The same goes for events. Bring your viewers to concerts, to premieres and to any other exciting events you might attend. In these cases, you can think of video as being a very natural extension to what you have previously been doing with your account – in this case, video will let your viewers almost *experience* that lifestyle you're promoting!

➤ Interviews – Let your visitors actually ask you questions and interact with you! Or how about conducting an interview with another personality and letting your viewers take part in that?

➤ Reviews and showcases – Got a product to promote? Why not showcase it *live*?

➤ Workouts

➤ Vlogs and discussions

Chapter 7

How to Create Stunning Pictures and Videos

As a very visual medium, it of course follows that you're going to need to learn to create some high quality pictures and videos if you really want to make a splash on Instagram. There is definitely an art to this and we're not going to be able to turn you into a pro photographer overnight... but there are certainly a few things we can do to help!

Hardware

Starting out, you might just want to upgrade your hardware. Of course, a good place to start is with a decent phone. While it is possible to take photos with cameras and then to add them to Instagram via your phone (which we'll get to in a moment), you are still going to need a good camera phone for your live videos at the very least. Good phones for this include the three newest Samsung Galaxies (the S6, S7 and S8 by the time many of you will be reading this) as well as the latest iPhones. Make sure that the selfie camera is good too. Samsungs are particularly good at this thanks to a particularly wide lens!

But for photos, it *does* make sense to take your pictures on a separate camera. If you can afford to get yourself a DSLR camera or *at least* a mirrorless camera, then you will find that you can take a significantly higher quality of photo and then use this to create the kind of professional sheen that otherwise wouldn't be possible.

There are a few other peripherals that you can get to help you along the way too. One is some form of lighting, such as a softbox. For video *and* for photos, having great lighting can make a *massive* difference to your picture quality. Meanwhile, you might also want to consider getting a lavmic to plug into your phone, which will greatly enhance your audio quality. For non-live video, you can use a Blue Yeti mic or another free-standing microphone for video that you upload later on.

Software can also make a big difference. I highly recommend the app Pixlr for making collages of your photos and you should also consider photo editing software for your PC. PhotoShop is of course the big one, but you can also do well with something like Gimp – which has the distinct advantage of being completely free!

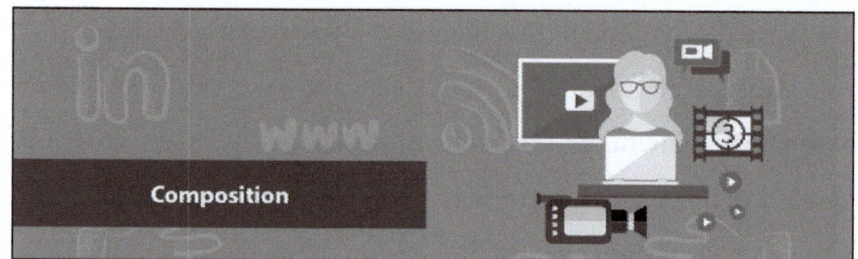

Composition

Perhaps more important than the hardware though is the wetware – the person behind the camera! There is definitely a skill to taking great photos and videos and this is something you'll learn with time.

I'm not going to go into how you achieve certain effects like macro effects here. That is up to you to learn and I highly recommend a photography course if you want to get good at Instagram. This will also teach you things like how to get the lighting just right so that your photo isn't too bright and you bring out the most detail with interesting shadows.

But for the meantime, just try to think about the foreground, the middle ground and the background. Give your photos depth by making sure that you have something of interest in all three stages and try to create a sense of scale by including more items than just the subject. Don't always take photos head on either, think about more interesting angles and perspectives.

More importantly, think about what you *aren't* photographing, or how you can set up a story. As I alluded to earlier in this book: an empty glass of wine can tell a story. Think about telling stories through omission – it's much more interesting than always tackling your subjects head on.

Chapter 8

Monetizing Your Instagram Account
and Finding Sponsors

So you've put in all this work to create a massive, powerful Instagram account. The next question is how you're actually going to profit from this and make money…

Promoting Your Own Products and Services

Of course, the most obvious method that will occur to the majority of internet marketers, is simply to have your own product or service to sell and to promote this *via* your Instagram. If you have a website where you sell products or where you sell services, then you can simply mention in your photos and videos and in your comments that people can check out your amazing offers over at your page. This works particularly well if you run discounts and include special offers through your channel. Likewise, you can feature the products *in* your pictures and your videos. Make sure that you offer value a lot of the time *without* promoting anything, and then when you do come to promote your products, you will find you have a good response.

To get this to work effectively, you need to align those value propositions. If you have a book on how to get fit, then it will sell much better when people realize that it contains the secrets that you followed in order to get the incredible body and enjoy the incredible workouts that you have been showcasing on your channel for so long.

Make sure as well to link your Instagram profile to your website and to tie the brand in closely. This way, people can discover you and become a fan on Instagram and then know where to go in order to find more of what you have to offer.

Finding Sponsors

Finding Sponsors

Another way to make money on Instagram though and the one that is perhaps most exciting for many people, is to find sponsors.

Finding sponsors on Instagram means that brands will pay you to post pictures wearing their clothes, drinking from their protein shakers, or working on their computers. You can get free stuff this way as well as some *big* amounts of money.

So how do you find these sponsors? One way is to go and check out sites that are designed to pair creators with sponsors. You can find this by heading over to Revfluence.com or Famebit.com… and there are many more sites just like this.

That's not how you land the *really* big sponsors though. To get those, you simply wait for them to contact you and once you get to a certain size, you can rest assured that this is going to happen.

To improve your chances, try to be present on more than one form of social media. Having a YouTube channel as well as an Instagram account will greatly boost your chances for example. Likewise, so too will having a Twitter account.

Having lots of followers is also essential and the more followers you have, the more you can charge.

On top of all this though, you should also make sure that your brand is consistent – that you have a consistent message and that you promote a positive message. You need to look professional and avoid slander or posting anything in poor taste. You need to represent the kind of brand that big companies are going to *want* to associate with.

CONCLUSIONS

There's a lot more to learn of course. You could benefit a great deal from a photography course as mentioned, learning to present yourself properly on video can help too, as can learning how to manage your other social media for maximum impact.

But at this point, you now know the most important basics. You know enough to get started. And you know enough to put you way ahead of the competition.

In short, the key to success on Instagram is to tell stories, to sell a dream and to promote a lifestyle that people want to be a part of. The new tools that Instagram has introduced provides you with more powerful ways to do this than ever before – by literally letting you speak directly to your audience, or to bring them along on your travels.

If you do this, then you'll find that Instagram can actually be more emotionally persuasive than practically any other form of social media. Combine that with all its amazing features and the sheer size of its audience and you have an incredibly opportunity that is just much too good to miss.

So what are you waiting for? Dive in and start telling your story!

Printed by Libri Plureos GmbH in Hamburg, Germany